Monographic Journals of the Near East

Afro-Asiatic Linguistics 1/1 (January 1974)

THE HAUSA ASPECT SYSTEM*

Paul Newman

and

Russell G. Schuh

Centre for the Study of Nigerian Languages
Ahmadu Bello University

In this paper the authors hope to account for the aspect marking constructions of modern Hausa by providing detailed historical explanations of their origin and development, beginning with morphological forms and syntactic patterns reconstructed for Proto-Hausa. The description accounts for the asymmetry in certain paradigms, the lack of parallelism between affirmative and negative paradigms in certain aspects, and some of the differences between contemporary dialects. The hypotheses about Hausa history are supported by reliable comparative data from other Chadic languages.

TABLE OF CONTENTS

*This paper is the outgrowth of a number of discussions between the authors, mostly during 1969-70 in the Northeast State of Nigeria. At that time both authors were engaged in field research supported by a National Science Foundation Grant, no. GS-2279 (Paul Newman, Principal Investigator). PN was working principally on Kanakuru, RGS on Ngizim, and it was through the study of these and other Chadic languages that the authors were able to gain fresh insights into the nature of Hausa structures. This paper has gone through several drafts, with useful comments provided by a number of scholars at all stages. In this connection, we would like to thank Herrmann Jungraithmayr, Roxana Ma Newman, and Raimo Anttila, to whom RGS submitted an early version as a course paper in a seminar on historical linguistics at UCLA. We would like especially to thank Claude Gouffé, not only for his discussion of the paper with PN, but also for his numerous valuable papers on the Hausa of Niger Republic.

1. INTRODUCTION

1.1 BACKGROUND

In Hausa, verb aspects[1] are differentiated on the surface by distinct sets of pronominal paradigms placed before the verb stem. In Yau da Gobe (Maxwell and Forshey n.d.), the popular pedagogical grammar used for years by missionaries and administrators in Nigeria, this feature of Hausa grammar is described as follows: "You must have a pronoun immediately before the

---

[1]The semantic nature of the categories in this dimension of the verbal system has been discussed by various writers, e.g. Klingenheben (1928/29), Parsons (1965), Gouffé (1966), Jungraithmayr (1968/69). The labels "tense," "aspect," and in some cases, "mode," have been used for the forms to be discussed. Since the topic of this paper is a formal characterization, with the semantic content being of only peripheral interest, we will use the term "aspect" to refer to all of the forms without laying strong claims to its semantic correctness in any particular case.

verb, no matter whether there is a noun subject or not. This is necessary because in Hausa the tense of the verb is shown by the pronoun" (p. 12). A similar statement precedes the description of the individual aspects in Abraham's more scholarly analytical/reference grammar (1959:6): "The root-form of the verb undergoes no change [except in the Continuous] but the various tenses are formed by placing different forms of pronouns before this root."[1] The pronouns mark the person, number, and, in the second and third persons singular, gender of the subject. In addition, each pronominal paradigm is distinguished from the others by some more or less constant feature such as vowel length or tone of the pronouns or special markers added to them. The nature of features that serve to distinguish the eight aspectual categories of Hausa are illustrated in the following table using the third person plural pronoun s u - as a model:

(1)   1. s ú - n   Perfective[2]
             2. s ú - k à   Relative Perfective (Perfective II)
             3. s ú - n à a   Continuous
             4. s ú - k è e   Relative Continuous (Continuous II)
             5. s ù   Subjunctive
             6. z á a - s ù   Future
             7. sᵂ á - à   Potential
             8. s ú - k à n   Habitual

The traditional means of accounting for these various pronominal forms has been simply to list full paradigms for each aspect. More recently two somewhat different variants of the transformational approach (Eulenberg 1967 and Gregersen 1967) have provided us with more productive ways of viewing the Hausa aspect system. The procedure followed in both of these accounts was to establish common underlying lexical forms for each of the person/number/ gender marking pronouns, to combine these underlying pronouns with special aspect formatives, and then to subject the combined forms to a series of morphophonemic rules whereby the various phonetic forms of the pronouns are obtained. The results of these transformational accounts have been only partly successful. They do correct the most glaring deficiencies of the traditional method, namely the failure to show cross-paradigmatic similarities and the underanalysis of morphologically complex, segmentable forms. Furthermore, by focussing on relations between forms rather than on surface detail of form, they have been able to capture significant generalizations about Hausa. The weakness of these accounts—stemming from an overly restricted, synchronic orientation—lies in the postulation of supposed relationships and morpho-syntactic rules that comparative evidence and further analysis show to be false.

The greatest contribution to our understanding of the nature and function of Hausa aspects is provided in an important series of articles by Gouffé (1964, 1966, 1966/67, 1967/68, 1968/69). Gouffé approaches the problem simultaneously from morphological, syntactic, and semantic points of view, and by careful analysis and imaginative interpretation he constructs a rich multi-dimensional picture of the Hausa aspect system. Depending heavily, as he does, on data from Western dialects, he is able to draw a fuller picture of the aspect system than the more usual, narrowly "Kano-centric" descriptions. Implicit in Gouffé's work is an appreciation of the fact that true understanding of the Hausa aspect system requires expansion of our vision both in space

---

[1] Actually verb stems do undergo changes of various sorts in Hausa (see Parsons 1960/61). What Abraham meant was that except for the Continuous aspect, which sometimes takes distinctive nominalized verbal forms, formal alternations in verb stems operate independently of aspect.

[2] The terminology that we have adopted is close to standard American usage (see Gregersen 1967, for example). These terms are intended simply as morpho-syntactic labels and not as exact semantic characterizations (see p. 2, fn. 1).

(dialectal) and in time (historical), and that our understanding of certain phenomena may have to await an historical description of their origins and development. Without the perspective of other Chadic languages, however, Gouffé's own attempts at historical explanation (based essentially on morpho-syntactic internal reconstruction) have been somewhat overly speculative and slightly off target.

Finally, we must mention the work of Jungraithmayr (1966, 1968/69, 1970a, 1970b) which has been so important in the development of this paper. The crux of Jungraithmayr's work has been the exemplification of the Hausa aspect system by placing it alongside that of closely related Chadic languages. Having looked at Hausa from a comparative vantage point, Jungraithmayr himself could not help but be impressed by the potential insights and understanding to be gained by this approach. "As far as I can see, the Hausa aspect system has not yet been considered in the light of corresponding aspectual situations in other West Chadohamitic languages . . . . Methodologically, such an historical approach is to be postulated before a final valuation of the Hausa aspect system can be attempted" (1968/69:16-17). Viewing Hausa from the perspective of other contemporary Chadic languages and of reconstructed West Chadic, Jungraithmayr has been able to spotlight those features of Hausa that are typically Chadic and those that are idiosyncratic. What needs to be added to Jungraithmayr's work is an appreciation of the dynamics involved in relating Hausa to these other languages and a creative picture of modern Hausa seen as the result of and as part of ongoing historical processes.

1.2   GOALS OF THE PRESENT STUDY

In the present paper we hope to account for the aspect marking constructions of modern Hausa by providing detailed historical explanations of their origin and development, beginning with morphological forms and syntactic patterns reconstructed for Proto-Hausa.[1] By utilizing historical depth and diachronic processes we have tried to provide a description of the present-day Hausa aspect system which accounts, among other things, for the asymmetry existing in certain paradigms, the lack of parallelism between the affirmative and negative paradigms in certain aspects, and some of the differences between contemporary dialects. Our attempt has been to provide a description that is coherent and comprehensive. Though this paper is necessarily speculative in places, we have tried throughout to support our hypotheses about Hausa history with reliable comparative data from other Chadic languages.

For purposes of this paper, we are distinguishing two major Hausa dialects. Standard Hausa, abbreviated SH (following Gouffé's HS for the French haoussa standard), refers to the dialect spoken in Kano and in the area fanning out eastward from that city. This is the dialect of Hausa used on Nigerian radio, in Hausa language newspapers in Nigeria, and in the standard dictionaries and grammars of Hausa. Western Hausa, abbreviated W, refers to dialects spoken in Niger and in general in most of the western and northern part of Hausaland. This designation lumps together the speech of Dogondoutchi (DD) and of Tibiri (T) described by Gouffé and Zima (1969).

In the examples a doubled vowel indicates a long vowel, a grave accent indicates low tone, and an acute accent high tone. Mid tones found in some Chadic languages (but not in Hausa) are left unmarked. Hyphens are used as needed to separate segmentable morphemes within what can be considered a single word. Occasional hypotheses advanced by one of the authors but not subscribed to by the other are indicated clearly either by [PN] or [RGS].

---

[1] Our "Proto-Hausa" reconstructions represent forms that we have good reason to postulate to be historical antecedents of modern Hausa forms which were already in the language before the differentiation of the present major dialects. How far back in time these reconstructions go, and how wide a time span is compressed under the term "Proto-Hausa" we cannot say.

2. THE CHADIC ASPECT MARKING SYSTEM

Before starting in with a description of Hausa, we must take a quick look at the situation else-where in Chadic, primarily limiting ourselves to the Plateau-Sahel branch of Chadic.[1] For Plateau-Sahel we can readily specify the basic traits of the aspect system along the lines suggested by Jungraithmayr (1968/69). In addition to the verb root itself, the typical nucleus of a verb phrase contains (a) a pronominal element (usually a short preverbal pronoun (PVP) but occasionally an independent pronoun), (b) an aspect morpheme (sometimes phonologically $\emptyset$), with or without (c) some change in the verb itself affecting either the tones or the vowels or both, e.g.

(2)   Sura: wurá   kə̀   náa   'she saw'
                      Ind-pn asp   verb
                      she   perf see

         Kanakuru: mə̀ $\emptyset$ tìlé   'we burnt (it)'
                      PVP   asp   verb
                      we   past burn

         Bolanci: ká $\emptyset$ pèté   'you should go out'
                      PVP   asp   verb + change (< pàtá)
                      you   subj go-out

Given this basic pn + asp + verb pattern for Plateau-Sahel, we are able to make additional specific claims about each of the three components.

2.1 THE PRONOMINAL ELEMENT

The first point to be emphasized is that the preverbal "subject" pronouns are reconstructed as having n o aspect marking function. This function was handled in Proto-Chadic by the special aspect marking morphemes and/or the verb stem changes. Related to the first point is the claim that these pronouns were generally invariant in shape. Some languages, for example Angas and languages closely related to it, do now mark aspectual differences by tone differences in these pronouns. We believe, however, that the tone differences (and those reported for preverbal pronouns in other Plateau-Sahel languages) were at one time non-distinctive. That is, these tone differences were originally conditioned by some other factor which was then lost, leaving only the tone of the pronoun as a marker of aspect. An example of the type of conditioning we are referring to is found in Ngizim (see Schuh 1971). In that language, the tones of the preverbal pronouns are normally polar to the following syllable. In the Perfective, which requires that the initial tone of the verb always be low—note the distinctive tonal marking of the verb stem —the pronoun is always high. By contrast, the Subjunctive allows verbs both with initial low tone and with initial high tone, the pronoun necessarily being high tone in constructions with the former, low tone with the latter. Thus, one finds a surface contrast with some verbs between high tone Perfective pronouns and low tone Subjunctive pronouns, despite the fact that the underlying tone of the pronouns used in both aspects is actually the same (polar).

---

[1] The Chadic subfamily of Afroasiatic has been classified as having two co-ordinate branches, Plateau-Sahel, which includes Hausa, and Biu-Mandara (see Newman and Ma 1966, and Hoffmann 1971). Within Plateau-Sahel, Hausa seems most closely related to the Bole and Angas groups, although its exact position is still uncertain.

Secondly, and here we have an important difference as compared with modern Hausa, third person pronouns were not used in constructions containing overt noun subjects. Thus Sura has màt-ni kð làa làa [woman-the perf bear child] 'the woman bore a child' not *màt-ni wurá kð làa làa (cf. example (2) above). We can go even further, moreover, and say that the typical rule in Plateau-Sahel in most aspects was not to use a third person pronoun (in the singular at least) whether a noun subject was used or not, e.g.

(3)   N   pn asp   verb

Ngizim: ∅ àa   ráwà   'he/she/they are running'

cf. Dðmzà   ∅ àa   ráwà   'Dðmza is running'

cf.   n-àa   ráwà   'I am running'

Karekare: ∅ ∅   shìndú-kò   'he/she stood up'

cf. Musa   ∅ ∅   shìndú-kò   'Musa stood up'

cf.   káø   shìndú-kò   'you (sg) stood up'

The actual forms of the preverbal pronouns for Proto-Plateau-Sahel are reconstructed roughly as follows:

(4)   1   *ni   1pl   *mu   [distinct 1pl exclusive and 1 dual as well?]

2m   *ka   2pl   *ku

2f   *ki

3m   (* si)   3pl   (* su)

3f   (* ta)

[Note: The third person pronouns were normally optionally or obligatorily omitted in verbal sentences.]

This reconstruction requires only a few minor comments: First note that the 3m pronoun is reconstructed as *si and not as *ya or *ni. The ya form used as subject pronoun for this person in modern Hausa is not found in other Chadic languages in any function and is not reconstructable for Chadic nor for the Plateau-Sahel branch of Chadic. The ni form of the 3m pronoun, while absent in Hausa, is found in most Chadic languages and is reconstructed for Proto-Chadic (cf. Kraft 1972).[1] It has not been included in the above paradigm for the following reason: although *si and *ni both existed in Proto-Chadic, only *si functioned as a PVP, *ni serving in object and complement positions. As far as the pronunciation of *si was concerned, it may have been [si], or it may have been [ši] with non-distinctive palatalization before the front vowel.

Turning to the first person plural, it is clear that at some level of depth in Chadic history one has to reconstruct 1pl inclusive vs. 1pl exclusive forms, and going even further back, probably

---

[1] The third masculine singular ni is found in fossilized constructions such wání "a certain . . . (m)" (cf. wátá "a certain . . . (f)', wású "certain . . . (pl)"). As we noted, the third masculine singular ya of Hausa is not reconstructable for Proto-Chadic. It is ironic that the existence of this "aberrant" PVP in Hausa was one of the first problems in the Hausa aspect system to attract our attention, yet it remains one of the few problems for which we have no really plausible solution. While we can remark on certain correlations of the ya pronominal element with other features of the aspect marking system (see section 3.1), we refrain from further speculation about the ultimate origin of ya in this paper.

a dual as well. Nevertheless, as a simplifying measure for the purpose of this paper, we will bypass the issue and include only one 1pl pronoun (*m u).

Finally, note that the absence of an impersonal pronoun in the reconstructed paradigm is intentional. Since modern Plateau-Sahel languages (other than Hausa) invariably employ other means of expressing impersonal subjects, it seems clear that the proto-language did not have a separate, distinct pronoun form corresponding to Hausa 'a (but see below, end of section 3.1).

2.2 ASPECT MARKERS

So far we have been able to reconstruct four aspect marking morphemes for Plateau-Sahel.[1] Since the presence of an overt marker in some aspects contrasts with absence of any overt marker in other aspects, we can treat phonological ϕ as itself being a marker. With this in mind, we can reconstruct the following: (1) *kà (or *kə̀), which indicated the Perfective; (2) and (3) ϕ, which was used both for a semantically less specific aspect labelled by German scholars as "Grundaspekt" and for the Subjunctive; and (4) *àa, which indicated the Imperfective (Continuous, Future, and/or Habitual depending on the language). The *kà Perfective form is still preserved in Hausa where it functions as the Relative Perfective marker (e.g. sú-kà, etc.). It is well documented in other Plateau-Sahel languages (e.g. Sura and Ron)[2] as well as in languages belonging to the Biu-Mandara Branch (e.g. Tera and Margi):

(5)   Sura: wurá kə̀ naa   'she saw'

          Ron (Fyer):   shí kà léf   'you (f.) have cut'

          Tera: tém wà masa[3]   'we bought (it)'

          Margi: nì gà wì   'I ran'

The "Grundaspekt with a ϕ aspect marker is extremely widespread in Chadic. The following examples glossed with a simple English past are typical:

(6)   Kanakuru: mə̀ àlí   'we saw (it)'

          Ron (Fyer):   shí léf   'you (f.) cut (it)'

          Ngizim: ná màsú   'I bought (it)'

In the Biu-Mandara branch of Chadic, the Subjunctive is often indicated by an overt marker (e.g. related forms of kə used in Tera, Margi, and Kotoko). In Plateau-Sahel, on the other hand, the Subjunctive, like the Grundaspekt, is usually marked by ϕ. (Where both aspects

---

[1] We are only talking about aspects for which we can reconstruct the actual shape of the markers. It is not yet clear exactly how many different aspectual categories were employed in Proto-Plateau-Sahel nor what they were.

[2] RGS believes that the marker k o (~ w o ~ ŋg o) which is suffixed to the verb in Karekare and Bolanci in the Perfective is etymologically related to the Chadic preverbal Perfective marker *kà, e.g. Karekare: ká shìnɗú-kò 'you (m) stood up'; Bolanci: mú básá-nì-wó 'we shot him'.

[3] The change of *k > y/w in Tera was presented cautiously in Newman and Ma (1966). Subsequent research has greatly strengthened our confidence in the historical reality of that correspondance.

coexist, other means, described in the following section, are used to distinguish between them.) Examples of Subjunctive marked by ∅ are plentiful, including Hausa, e.g.

(7)	Hausa:	dóolè kù fìtá	'you (pl) must go out'
	Bolanci:[1]	kádàa mú ɓòlté sá	'lest we break it'
	Sura:	(ni rét kú) rá jì	'(it is good) that she come'
	Ron (Fyer):	shì ɗut	'that she ask'

The Imperfective marker *àa, usually represented by a pronominal of the form Càa, is best illustrated by the Hausa Negative Continuous forms (báa-tàa, báa-sᵂàa, etc.) and by the following examples from Ngizim and Karekare:

(8)	Ngizim:	n-àa kácí	'I will return/am returning'
		àa láunà-gâa	'he/she/they will see me/are looking at me'
	Karekare:	n-àa bádú-yì	'I am kicking (it)'
		kᵂ-áa dábú-yì	'you (pl.) are breaking (it)'

In addition to true aspect morphemes, many Chadic languages also make use of quasi-aspect marking morphemes derived from the names for body parts in conjunction with one aspect marker or another, e.g.

(9)	Angas:	ŋán pò sé	'I am eating'	(< pò 'mouth')
	Bolanci:	ísíŋ kó pètè	'he is going out'	(< kó 'head')
	Sura:	wurá-ŋ káà sé	'she is eating'	(< káà 'head')
	Ngizim:	náa tèkà wánà	'I am working'	(< tèkà 'body')

The Hausa Habitual marker, kàn, possibly owes its origin in a similar manner to the body part term káì 'head'.[2]

2.3 STEM CHANGES

The third type of marking associated with aspectual differences in Chadic is a change in the verb itself. Two such verb stem changes can be tentatively reconstructed: a change in the final vowel of the verb to *i or (*e) in the Subjunctive; and the formation of "habituative stems" (= "Habitativstamm") by expansion of the basic form of the verb through suffixation or infixation of *awa (cf. Jungraithmayr 1966).[3]

---

[1] Most of the Bolanci examples cited in this paper are taken from field notes of PN on the dialect of the Gombe area. For further information on Bolanci already in print, see Lukas (1970-72).

[2] In our opinion this is a much more reasonable explanation than the hypothesis advanced by Klingenheben (1928/29: 258n) and adopted by Jungraithmayr (1968/69: 21n) which relates the Hausa habitual marker kàn to an Efik verb kam meaning 'to use to do something'.

[3] The infixal and suffixal stem formatives may well have been functionally distinct, the one creating the true Habituative stem, the other forming gerundives. This would not, however, alter our basic analysis; it would only require that we delete some examples.

The formation of Subjunctive stems by vowel fronting can be illustrated by Ngizim and Bolanci:

(10)

	Basic form	Subjunctive form	
Ngizim:	káasə	káasí [káašíi]	'to sweep'
	zə̀ba	zə̀bì	'to marry'
Bolanci:	pórú	pòrí	'to say'
	wùndú	wùndé	'to call'
	básáa	bèsé	'to shoot'

This alternation has been lost in Hausa.

The old habituative stem formation has been widely retained throuthout Plateau-Sahel (including Hausa) under a variety of guises and surface manifestations, e.g.

(11)

	Basic form	Habituative stem		Present-day usage
Hausa:	kóomà	kóomàa-ẁáa	'return'	Continuous
Mubi:	tì i	tú-wà	'eat'	Habitual
Kanakuru:	pòrí	pór-má	'go out'	Continuous/Future
Bolanci:	ɗìnkú	ɗínk-ó/ɗínk-ò̀o	'cook'	Habitual
Ron (Daffo):	m o t	mwaát	'die'	Habitual
Ron (Bokkos):	c u	cwááy/cwayì	'eat'	Habitual/Continuous

3.   THE HAUSA SYSTEM

In Hausa a number of independent developments and realignments have taken place that make it look different in some respects from its close relatives; nevertheless, the general character of the Chadic aspect marking system is still recoverable. We will begin our account of Hausa with a reconstruction of the basic, unmarked preverbal pronoun paradigm. We will then turn to the individual aspects of modern Hausa and demonstrate how the modern paradigmatic sets can be derived from an immediately antecedent PVP + asp + verb system similar to what we described above in general terms for Plateau-Sahel.

3.1   RECONSTRUCTION OF THE PROTO-HAUSA PREVERBAL PRONOUNS

For Proto-Hausa we reconstruct the following PVP paradigm:

(12)

1	*nì	1pl	*mù
2m	*kà	2pl	*kù
2f	*kì		
3m	*sì	3pl	*sù
3f	*tà		

This set is identical (except for the addition of tone) to paradigm (4) reconstructed earlier for Proto-Plateau-Sahel and virtually identical to the pronoun set adopted as underlying forms by Gregersen (1967) in a synchronic, generative description of Hausa.[1] Having set up a single pronoun paradigm with low tone for all aspects (abbreviated P̀r by him), Gregersen proposes a synchronic tone raising rule to account for surface PVP's with high tone such as mú-nàa 'we continuous' and mú-kàn 'we habitual'. This rule is stated as follows (minus a few details irrelevant to the present discussion):

(13)   P̀r → Ṕr / —— + Aspect (where Aspect ≠ àa, 'Negative Continuous')

Note that as formulated by Gregersen, the tone change is completely conditioned by the presence or absence of a morphological category, "Aspect."

While we agree with Gregersen on the need for a raising mechanism, we would suggest the following as a better formulation of the rule:

(14)   P̀r → Ṕr / —— [. . . V̌ . . .]$_{\text{Aspect}}$

That is, a low tone preverbal pronoun (P̀r) is dissimilated to high tone before a low tone aspect marker.[2] The category Aspect is still mentioned, but the inclusion of phonological conditioning for the tone change is intrinsically more natural and more in character with tonal assimilation and dissimilation rules affecting these pronouns in other Chadic languages. The category Aspect, moreover, might not even have to be mentioned if Pr + Aspect were said to form a single word — a claim which is independently motivated — and the tone dissimilation were said to operate only within a word. The following aspects illustrate the operation of rule (14):[3]

(15)   Relative Perfective: sù + kà   →   sú-kà

            Continuous: sù + nàa   →   sú-nàa

            Relative Continuous: sù + kèe   →   sú-kèe

            Potential: sù + àa   →   sʷáà (→ sáà for some speakers)

            Habitual: sù + kàn   →   sú-kàn

Aspects not subject to rule (14) where the underlying low tone appears on the surface are the Subjunctive (sù), the Negative Perfective (bà-sù . . . bá) and the Future (záa-sù).

Note that our analysis permits us to treat the Subjunctive as a true aspect with a phonologically ∅ marker whereas Gregersen's rule requires that the Subjunctive be considered as something ·

---

[1] Gregersen erroneously postulates *mi as the underlying form for the first person singular, otherwise the forms in his paradigm are identical to ours. Klingenheben (1928/29) also lists a similar paradigm but does not mark tone.

[2] Gouffé (1966/67: 54) correctly recognized that the sequence of high tone PVP plus low tone aspect marker was not an arbitrary sequence but rather constituted "une manifestation du phénomène, bien connu en haoussa de 'polarité tonale'...".

[3] For the moment, we will leave open the question whether the operations illustrated in (15) are part of a synchronic description of Hausa or a diachronic account of how Hausa got to be the way it is.

other than an aspect. (Otherwise the pronouns would be subject to his rule and end up with high tone.) Similarly, Gregersen's rule requires that the aspectual category Perfective be deleted in the negative Perfective (bà-sù . . . bá) in order to keep the low tone on the PVP's whereas it is evident on semantic and syntactic grounds that what is missing in the Negative Perfective is an overt aspect marker, not the aspect category itself.

Gregersen's rule, (13), does appear to account for one aspect paradigm that our rule, (14) fails to properly account for. That is the Perfective pronouns táa, sún, etc. It would not be unreasonable to propose an underlying /tà-á/, /sù-ń/, etc. with the normal PVP followed by a high tone Perfective aspect morpheme having allomorphs /á/ or /ń/, conditioned by features of person, number, and gender. (This is essentially Gregersen's proposal.) Gregersen's rule would then apply to raise the tone of the pronoun before any aspect marker, giving the correct surface forms with all high tone.[1] Regardless of any synchronic merits that this proposal may have, it is wrong as a historical explanation for the high tone of the Perfective pronouns. In fact, the pronouns in the Perfective aspect have an entirely different origin in Hausa, outside the aspect system, i.e. they are not composed of the historical PVP plus an aspect marker (see sec. 4.1). Rather than being counterexamples to our rule (14), they simply have nothing to do with that rule.

It follows from our general analysis and that of Gregersen that the PVP's themselves have no intrinsic aspect marking function and that the surface tones found on the PVP's, whether high or low, are of no deep significance. Though used in the Subjunctive without an overt aspect marker, the PVP's in paradigm (12) are not in themselves Subjunctive pronouns. Gouffé, for example, makes this incorrect identification and thus is led into the untenable position of claiming that the Future and the Negative Perfective, which also use the unmarked PVP set, bear a special syntactic and semantic relationship to the Subjunctive (Gouffé 1966, 1967/68).

Leaving aside the matter of tone, paradigm (12) requires a few other comments. For dialectal and comparative reasons, the first person singular PVP has to be reconstructed as *ni, of which the surface forms ni/'n/'in/n are merely non-distinctive phonological variants. The SH form ná used in ná-kèe, ná-kàn, etc. probably represents a replacement of the true PVP *ni by a form taken from the Perfective and Relative Perfective paradigms (see sec. 4.1). The 3m form is still reconstructed as *sì (as was the case for Proto-Plateau-Sahel) rather than *yà in spite of the predominant use of the latter form as the 3m preverbal pronoun in modern SH.

While our thoughts about the origin of ya are still too speculative to present here (cf. p. 6, fn. 1) we can say something about its incorporation into Hausa. The early substitution of yà for *sì as a 3m PVP only affected those fused aspect pronouns of the form Caa now represented by yáa Perfective, yáà Potential, and yàa Negative Continuous (in SH only). The Relative Perfective yá (SH) / yáC (W) also goes back to a form containing *yáa (see sec. 6.2). This development must have taken place very early in Hausa linguistic history as its effects are seen in all Hausa dialects. Much later, after the differentiation of the present dialects, a second and independent development took place, but only in SH. Here we find the adoption of yà as a true PVP in all aspects resulting in the complete replacement of the older pronoun shì in its preverbal functions. Cf. the following:

(16)   SH   W

    yá-nàa fìtáa   =   shí-nàa hìtáa   'he is going out'

    dóolè yà tàfí   =   dóolè shì tàhí   'he must go'

---

[1] Actually, Gregersen's rule raising pronoun tone would not be needed here. Leben (1971) presents good evidence, on purely phonological grounds, that a sequence low-high on a single syllable is changed to high. Thus, /tà-á/ would automatically be converted to [táa], and the internal structure of the syllable would be irrelevant.

This sequence can be diagrammed as follows:

(17)   Stage I   Stage II

         (Early Hausa)

$$\text{SH} \begin{cases} \text{*yáa} > \text{yáa (no change)} \\ \text{*shì} > \text{yà} \end{cases}$$

$$\begin{cases} \text{*sáa} > \text{yáa} \\ \text{*shì} > \text{shì (no change)} \end{cases}$$

$$\text{W} \begin{cases} \text{*yáa} > \text{yáa (no change)} \\ \text{*shì} > \text{shì (no change)} \end{cases}$$

NB: The symbol > here indicates morphological replacement, not phonological change.

Finally, there is the question of the indefinite "pronoun" 'a found in all aspects of contemporary Hausa, e.g. Perfective 'án, Continuous 'á-nàa, Future záa-'à, etc. While other Chadic languages do not have an indefinite pronominal subject form corresponding phonologically to Hausa 'à,[1] the Hausa form can still be traced back to a Plateau-Sahel morpheme. In some languages closely related to Hausa, and, we suggest, in Pre-Hausa, there is a third person preverbal "place holder" of the form a used in some aspects. Examples of this place holding a in Kanakuru can be seen below in (20). In Kanakuru, its use has been limited to the singular, but in Bolanci, it is found in both singular and plural (cf. Lukas, 1970-72, section 15). Though this a appears to occupy the position of the preverbal pronouns, it is demonstrably not pronominal. First, it appears even when preceded by a nominal subject. Moreover, a simple a is found nowhere in Chadic in a third person pronominal function in other syntactic environments.

As pointed out in section 2.1, comparative evidence shows that in Proto-Plateau-Sahel, no preverbal pronouns were used when there was an overt noun subject. Clearly then, Hausa has innovated by making the use of the preverbal pronouns obligatory in all environments (with the exception of the Continuous after a noun subject). After the presence of the preverbal pronouns was made obligatory for definite third person subjects, the *'à place holder was available to indicate indefinite subjects, where features of number and gender were unspecified. While *'à in Pre-Hausa was probably limited to certain aspects and functioned in part as an aspect marker for third person, its new primary function as an indefinite subject marker freed it from any specific aspect marking function. It was thus extended to use in all aspects.

The indefinite 'a patterns with the plural preverbal pronouns by virtue of its adding -n in the Perfective (cf. the paradigms in (18) below). It is not certain why this is so, though it is possible that 'a replaced an earlier means of marking indefinite subjects that already required plural concord.

---

[1] This is not meant to imply that indefinite subject pronouns are not found elsewhere in Plateau-Sahel. Ngizim, for example, has a form ndà used exactly as Hausa 'à. Moreover, ndà undergoes all the same tonal and vowel length modifications as the regular person marking preverbal pronouns of Ngizim. Etymologically, ndà is the common Chadic word for 'people', and indeed it is used in this meaning in Ngizim. Thus, while it might be possible to reconstruct Proto-Plateau-Sahel as having some syntactic device for marking indefinite subjects of verbs, we cannot at this time assert what the specific form of that device was.

4. THE HAUSA PERFECTIVE ASPECT

The present day pronoun paradigms for this aspect are as follows:

(18)   SH   W   NEG (SH and W)

1   náa   náa   bà-n . . . bá[1]

2m   káa   káa   . . . kà . . . .

2f   kín   kyáa/kée   . . . kì . . . .

3m   yáa   yáa   . . . y . . . .

3f   táa   táa   . . . tà . . . .

1pl   mún   mún   . . . mù . . . .

2pl   kún   kún   . . . kù . . . .

3pl   sún   sún   . . . sù . . . .

4pl   'án   'án   . . . 'à . . . .

At first glance the Perfective pronouns listed above appear to be unitary forms that do not conform to the typical Hausa/Chadic pattern in which aspect is indicated by a short vowel PVP plus an overt aspect marker. They can, however, be analyzed to so conform. Gregersen (1967), for example, treats the initial CV of these forms as the PVP and the final n and : (vowel length) as allomorphs of a separable Perfective marker. This analysis, however, leaves a lot of questions unanswered.

In the first place, there is the question of the strange n ~ : suppletion not evidenced elsewhere in Hausa. Secondly, if one considers these forms to contain the usual PVP's, it is odd that yáa should be the 3m Perfective pronoun used in all Hausa dialects when in dialects other than SH, the normal, unmarked 3m PVP is shi, not ya. Thirdly, there is the problem of the relation between the affirmative and negative paradigms. In order to account for these anomalies it is necessary to set aside the type of synchronic analysis adopted by Gregersen and seek an explanation for the present-day Perfective paradigms in terms of reconstructable historical developments. The following represents such an analysis.

4.1 ORIGIN OF THE HAUSA PERFECTIVE PRONOUNS

For Proto-Hausa we reconstruct the Perfective on the model of the Grundaspekt in related languages, with the short, lowtone PVP's plus a ϕ marker:

(19)   1   *nì   1pl   *mù

2m   *kà   2pl   . *kù

2f   *kì

3m   —   3pl   (*sù)

3f   —

_____

[1]In Hausa negatives formed with bà . . . bá, the first bà goes immediately before the PVP while the second bá is placed at the end of the predicate. The various forms of the negative markers are described in Newman (1971a).

Compare paradigm (19) with the following Perfective paradigm in Kanakuru:

(20)   nà tùpé   'I sent (it)'   mə̀ tùpé   'we sent (it)'

        kà . . .   'you (m) . . .'   kə̀ . . .   'you (pl) . . .'

        shì . . .   'you (f) . . .'

        φ à . . .   'he . . .'   wù . . .   'they . . .'

        φ à . . .   'she . . .'

Also interesting is a comparison between the forms reconstructed for Proto-Hausa with sentences from contemporary Gwandara, a language so close to Hausa that it almost qualifies as a Hausa dialect:[1]

(21)   ni tsa ji jiya   'I went home yesterday' (= SH na je gida jiya)

        mu gba duwa   'we shot an elephant'

        wu sa giya mama   'they drank all the beer'

In Proto-Hausa the difference between the Perfective and the Subjunctive must have been marked by some kind of change in the verb stem, either tonal or vocalic or both. Cf. the following:

(22)   Perfective   Subjunctive

    Kanakuru: nà tùpé 'I sent (it)'   . . . nà túpé '. . . that I send (it)'

               mə̀ ɗə̀hí 'we built (it)'   . . . me ɗə̀hí '. . . that we build (it)'

    Bolanci: nì pùushú sùɓà   . . . nì pùushé sùɓà

                'I washed a gown'   '. . . so that I wash a gown'

               nì básáa kwàmì   . . . nì bèsé kwàmì

                'I shot a cow'   '. . . so that I shoot a cow'

As indicated by the reconstruction in (19), we are assuming that Proto-Hausa had strict limitations on the use of third person PVP's. More specifically , it seems clear that third person PVP's were not allowed in sentences with expressed noun subjects whether singular or plural. When no noun subject was expressed, a third person PVP was probably optionally used in the plural but still not allowed in the singular. Again, we can cite examples from Gwandara to illustrate what the proto-language may have looked like:

(23)   Adamu ka ku   'Adamu caught a rat' (= SH Adamu ya kama kusu)

        mace ci to   'the woman ate tuwo '

Where, then, did the Hausa Perfective pronouns (paradigm (18)) come from? When we look at other Chadic languages we discover that similar pronoun sets exist but n o t functioning as preverbal aspect pronouns. Rather, these pronouns normally constitute what one might call a "free set," functioning in general as non-bound direct objects, as objects of prepositions, as

---

[1] The Gwandara examples are all taken from unpublished field notes of PN collected during a brief stopover in Karshi, a village area some 60 miles south of Jos on the Makurdi road.

subjects or objects of equational sentences, or other "unbound" functions, depending on the language. Consider, for example, the following paradigm of direct object pronouns in Karekare:[1]

(24)   1   nàa   1pl   múnàa

        2m   kàa   2pl   kúnàa

        2f   càa

        3m   sàa   3pl   súnàa

        3f   tàa

What is particularly interesting about the above paradigm as compared with the Hausa Perfective paradigm (18) is that the singular pronouns all contain a long vowel (specifically long aa) and that the plural pronouns all contain an n as C_2, i.e. the same $n \sim :$ suppletive alternation that has been described as constituting the Perfective morpheme in Hausa. When we look further in Chadic, we discover that non-subject plural pronouns with final -n are to be found in Sura, Ron, Kanakuru, and Jegu, among others. Thus on comparative grounds, it is evident that the final -n in the Hausa Perfective pronouns mun, kun, and sun is in origin a plural marker, not an aspect marker.

While we might reconstruct an archetypical paradigm of pronouns with the form *CV for Proto-Plateau-Sahel (and probably Proto-Chadic) it is evident that for unbound functions we must reconstruct the pronouns as having been augmented: basically, the augment consisted of vowel length in the singular, *-nV or *-n in the plural. Indeed, an n element associated with plural pronouns is a feature of Afroasiatic languages other than Chadic (cf. Lukas 1937/38).

In many languages, including Hausa, the unbound pronouns have become frozen and their pronoun-plus-augment analysis has been obscured, giving simply "long" pronoun paradigms alongside "short" paradigms deriving from the unaugmented bound forms. Not infrequently we find "long" and "short" pronoun forms alternating depending on syntactic position or function. In such cases, we can fairly safely reconstruct the "long" alternate as deriving from the use in that position of the free pronoun forms at an earlier stage of the language, even if this is not entirely evident on language internal grounds. We will see that this is true, with some qualifications, for the Hausa Perfective pronouns.

As a further example of "long" and "short" forms in alternation, consider the following Kanakuru data:

(25)   mə̀ də̀lə̀ wúní   'we pushed them'   [d. o. - long form]

        mə̀ də́l-wù métə́kà   'we pushed a car for them'   [i. o. - short form]

        lówòi gə̀n kái   'the boy and you'   [disjunctive - long form]

        kà tùpè lówòi   'you sent the boy'   [Perf. PVP - short form]

Returning now to the Hausa Perfective Paradigm of (18), we note that the "obvious" identification of -n as a plural marker has been obscured up to now primarily because of the presence in the paradigm of the second person feminine form kín. As long as this -n was thought to be the same as the one in the plural forms mun/kun/sun, there was no way to arrive at the

---

[1] Specifically, this is the set used with verbs in the Perfective. In other aspects slightly different variants of these pronouns are used. This paradigm, taken from field notes of Maxine Schuh, is identical to that provided by Lukas (1970-72, sec. 178) but without tone.

correct analysis. Comparative evidence shows, however, that the identity of the final nasal of k í n and that of the plural forms is completely fortuitous. The nasals have separate origins and the present confusion is simply due to the neutralization in syllable final position of m and n. Unlike the plural forms, which are reconstructable with an *-n, the free form of the 2f pronoun must be reconstructed as *kVm. Support for this reconstruction is provided by paradigms such as the following:

(26)		Ngizim	Burrum	Budduma
	1	í y û	' a m	- n i
	2m	c ì	g a	- g u
	2f	k ә̀ m	g a m	- g e̦ m
	3m	á c ì	t a a	- n e̦
	3f	á t û	s a a	- -

The *-m in the second person feminine has been widely lost in Chadic by analogic leveling with the other singular pronouns, none of which contained a final nasal, e.g. Karekare c à a instead of *c ә̀ m and the W Hausa Perfective k y á a instead of SH k í n.   Nevertheless, its existence as illustrated above in widely disparate subgroups of Chadic shows that it must be reconstructed for all of Chadic. It must even represent a retention from a period of Afroasiatic prior to the Chadic split since the -m is still seen, for example, in the Berber languages.

We have now identified -n as a component of plural pronouns, -m as a component of the second person feminine singular, length as an integral component of the other singular pronouns, and the whole SH paradigm (18) as originally being a basic free set. What remains to be explained is how this set came to be used before verbs in Hausa and thus became transformed into a bound, preverbal aspect marking set. Although details are left to be worked out, we can suggest an outline of the general nature of the developments that must have taken place.

At the very beginning of this section we indicated that Proto-Hausa probably used no overt pronoun in the third person singular even when a noun subject was not expressed. Such pronoun-less sentences would thus have been ambiguous from the point of view of gender. This hypothetical state of affairs can be illustrated by present-day Karekare.

(27)	n à ŋ g à t á a k ò	'I fell down'	m ú ŋ g à t - á n k ò	'we fell down'
	k á . . .	'you (m) . . .'	k ú . . .	'you (pl) . . .'
	c í . . .	'you (f) . . .'		
	ɸ ŋ g à t á a k ò	'he/she . . .'	(s ú) . . .	'they . . .'

The PVP in the third person plural is optional in sentences with no noun subject. Even when the PVP is not used, a sentence with a plural subject can be unambiguously interpreted because of the plural suffix -a n on the verb. In the singular, however, a third person PVP is not allowed. If one wants to disambiguate ŋ g à t á a - k ò and indicate whether the subject is masculine or femine, then one must use a free pronoun, e.g.

(28)	s à a ŋ g à t á a - k ò	'he fell down'
	t à a ŋ g à t á a - k ò	'she fell down'

It seems likely that Proto-Hausa used third person free pronouns in place of ɸ in the subject slot in exactly the same way that Karekare now does, the difference being that early in

Hausa their use became obligatory.[1] Marking of subject plurality by verb-stem suffixation was probably lost very early in the history of Hausa, if it was a feature of Proto-Hausa at all. The use of an overt pronoun in the third person would have therefore been necessary to avoid ambiguity of number as well as of gender. Whether Hausa used a normal PVP in the third person plural in the Perfective (as Karekare allows) or whether from the beginning it only allowed a free pronoun in the plural as well as in the singular is not clear.

After the incorporation of the third person pronouns as obligatory members of the set, the paradigm used in the Perfective would have been as follows (cf. paradigms 18 and 19):

(29)   1   *nì   1pl   *mù

          2m   *kà   2pl   *kù

          2f   *kì

          3m   *sáa (> *yáa)   3pl   *sún (or *sù?)

          3f   *táa

Paradigm (29), being composed partly of simple PVP's and partly of free pronouns obviously lacked the stability of a balanced symmetrical pronoun set. It thus gave way to a new set modeled after the third person pronouns in which the first and second pronouns were also replaced by free forms. The leveling may also have been stimulated by analogy with the Relative Perfective pronouns which at that time were probably formed with free pronouns plus the suffix kà (see sec. 6.2). Also, it is likely that the changes in the verb stem itself which had distinguished the Perfective from the Subjunctive were in the process of disappearing and that the complete replacement of the unmarked PVP in the Perfective by another set served to keep these two aspects apart. Thus, the free pronouns, which were originally reintroduced in verbal constructions to distinguish gender (and probably number) in the third person, ended up as aspect markers, unambiguously representing the Perfective as opposed to other aspects.

4.2 NEGATIVE PERFECTIVE

The process whereby free pronouns came to be the present-day Perfective set only affected constructions in the affirmative. The Negative Perfective has retained the Perfective pattern reconstructed for Proto-Hausa namely PVP + ϕ aspect marker, i.e.

(30)   bà kà káamà kàazáa bá   'you didn't catch a hen'

          < *kà ϕ káamà kàazáa   'you caught a hen'

                                         + the negative bà . . . bá (cf. p. 13, fn. 1)

The form of the pronouns used in the present-day Negative Perfective is due to the above, very simple, straightforward historical explanation. It should be emphasized again that it is n o t due to any synchronic connection between the Negative Perfective and the Subjunctive as postulated by Parsons (1965:11) and Gouffé (1966:164n).

A special note of interest here is that in the Perfective as in the Continuous (described in section 7) it is the negative form that has been most conservative and gives us the best picture of historical antecedents and the affirmative constructions that have been most innovative.

---

[1] This statement applies to constructions without noun subjects. The use of PVP's with overt noun subjects must have come in even later.

5. THE SUBJUNCTIVE ASPECT

The paradigm used for the Subjunctive in modern Hausa is as follows:

(31)   1   'ǹ (SH) / 'in (W)   1pl   mù

            2m   kà   2pl   kù

            2f   kì

            3m   yà (SH) /shì (W)   3pl   sù

            3f   tà   4pl   'à

The Negative Subjunctive is formed by placing the marker kádà/káȓ in SH, káɗ in W, before the pronouns in paradigm (31), e.g. (SH) kádà kà fìtá, (W) káȓ kà hìtá 'don't go out'.

The pronouns used in the Subjunctive are simply the bare preverbal pronouns. The only changes from the reconstructed paradigm (12) are the first person metathesis or apocope *ni > ìn or *ni > ǹ (thence to 'ìn or 'ǹ) and the replacement in SH of *sì by yà. As in the case of the Negative Perfective where aspect is also marked by ɸ , the PVP's in the Subjunctive retain the underlying low tone in contrast to an aspect such as the Continuous which employs exactly the same pronoun set but with automatically conditioned high tone (e.g. mú-nàa < *mù-nàa, cf. Subjunctive mù and Negative Perfective bà mù . . . bá). As mentioned earlier, the Subjunctive was undoubtedly overtly marked in Proto-Hausa but by some kind of change in the verb stem, such as one finds in Ngizim and Bolanci (cf. example 10), rather than by a separate aspect marker. Due to the loss of these aspectual verb stem changes in modern Hausa, the Subjunctive has become a formally unmarked aspect, leading some scholars to the erroneous opinion that the Subjunctive is not an aspect in its own right (cf. Eulenberg 1967 and Gregersen 1967). The historical/comparative evidence, however, supports Gouffé's contention—argued on synchronic grounds—that the Hausa Subjunctive should be considered an aspect on a par with the others.[1]

As far as the Negative Subjunctive is concerned, we need only summarize briefly what has been explained in detail elsewhere (Newman 1971a). In Proto-Hausa, the Negative Subjunctive was formed by a regular affirmative Subjunctive construction preceded by a semantically negative adverbial LEST (represented in modern Hausa by kádà and its variants) and followed by the true negative marker bá. In sentences containing LEST, this final bá could be deleted. Sometime in early Hausa, before the differentiation of the present dialects, the use of the final bá was discontinued entirely and the use of LEST in negative constructions became obligatory.

---

[1]Part of Gouffé's motivation for introducing the term "aoriste" for the commonly used "subjunctive" was to mark "l'intégration de cette série au système proprement aspectuel du verbe haoussa" (1966:158).

6.   THE RELATIVE PERFECTIVE

The Relative Perfective paradigms for SH and W dialects of Hausa are as follows:

(32)   SH   W
        1   ná   níC
        2m   ká   káC
        2f   kí-kà   kíC (kín-kà)
        3m   yá   yáC (shín-kà)
        3f   tá   táC
        1pl   mú-kà   mún-kà
        2pl   kú-kà   kún-kà
        3pl   sú-kà   sún-kà
        4pl   'á-kà   'án-kà

(Capital C indicates a doubling of the following consonant.)

6.1   USE OF THE RELATIVE PERFECTIVE AND ITS PROTO-HAUSA FORM

The Relative Perfective in Hausa is used in place of the Perfective in relative clauses or when a question word or emphasized constituent is to the left of the verb.[1] Obligatory replacement of a neutral Perfective in these contexts by a special Perfective form is also found in languages as distant from Hausa and from each other as Kanakuru (Plateau-Sahel) and Tera (Biu-Mandara). Although it is not yet possible to identify what the actual marking of the Proto-Chadic Relative Perfective must have been, the existence of the transformation in Proto-Chadic is quite certain.

The Hausa Relative Perfective is characterized in some persons by a suffix -kà. This form has been reconstructed in Chadic as a marker for the Perfective, not the Relative Perfective; nevertheless the uniformity of the rules governing the uses of the Perfective and Relative Perfective forms in all Hausa dialects and the regular differences in phonological representation indicate clearly that the morpheme -kà must have already been established as a marker of relative contexts by the time of Proto-Hausa.

6.2   DEVELOPMENT OF THE RELATIVE PERFECTIVE FORMS

For Proto-Hausa Relative Perfective we reconstruct the following forms composed of the reconstructed free pronoun set plus the relative marker -kà:

---

[1] Use of the Relative Perfective in sequential contexts in Hausa appears to be an independent development. Other Chadic languages have a sequential aspect, but none that we are aware of use the Relative Perfective in that way.

(33)   1   *náa-kà   1pl   *mún-kà

          2m   *káa-kà   2pl   *kún-kà

          2f   *kín-kà

          3m   *sáa-kà (> *yáa-kà) 3pl   *sún-kà

          3f   *táa-kà

Reconstruction (33) embodies two explicit claims, namely (1) that -kà was originally used in all persons and not just in some persons as we find in contemporary Hausa, and (2) that the Relative Perfective made use of the long free pronoun set (as in W mún-kà) rather than the short PVP set (as suggested by SH mú-kà). We believe that paradigm (33) represents the true antecedent of the modern Relative Perfective forms because it permits us to provide a natural and coherent explanation not only for the differences that exist between dialects but also for the suppletion found within each dialect.

The historical developments leading from the forms in (33) to the contemporary forms in (32) involved what were essentially minor phonological changes accompanied by various analogical realignments. The following represents a chronologically ordered sequence of developments:

(34)   ⎧ Vowel Apocope: *táa-kà > *táa-k (>*tá-k)
          all   ⎪   (But not   *sún-kà ≯ *sún-k)
          dialects   ⎨ Gemination: *tá-k > táC
                          ⎩
          SH only   ⎧ Degemination: *táC > tá
                          ⎨ Analogical loss of -n: *sún-kà > sú-kà
                          ⎩

Vowel Apocope

This early change resulted in the loss of the vowel from the aspect marker -kà when attached to pronouns of the phonological shape *Cáa, such as náa, káa, yáa, and táa, but not kín or sún. The shortening of the pronominal vowel from áa to á (in *táak > ták) was due to a syllable overload rule still functional in Hausa which shortens long vowels and diphthongs in closed syllables. The application of the vowel apocope rule to the *CV̂N-kà pronouns such as kín-kà, sún-kà, etc. was blocked by rigid phonological constraints in Hausa against syllables of the form *CVCC.[1]

Gemination

The syllable final k left by vowel apocope came to be realized not as a simple consonant but as a more abstract phonological unit C which completely assimilates to all following consonants. This is evidenced today in W dialect forms of the Relative Perfective derived from *Cák (in turn from *Cáa-kà), e.g. yàushè káz zákàa? 'when did you come?', (< káC zákàa), wàndà níg gánii 'what I saw', (< níC gáníi). The change from *nak > *ník > níC is presumably a relatively late change in W, supported by the *i of the first person singular preverbal pronoun *nì > 'ǹ or 'iǹ and by the independent pronoun níi.

The change from *k > C perhaps requires some further justification. In a well-known sound change, first documented by Klingenheben (1927-28), syllable final velars > w. Thus,

_____

[1] See Newman (1972) for a discussion of constraints on syllable weight which block syllables of the shape *CVVC or *CVCC.

*ɓáknáa > ɓáunáa 'bush cow' (cf. plural ɓákàanée). This sound change must have happened early in the history of Hausa, since it has affected all dialects uniformly. Why, then, did *nák, *kák, etc. not become *náu, *káu, etc.? The answer is that the syllable final velar > w change had run its course and was no longer a productive process at the time of vowel apocope in the Relative Perfective pronouns. Rather, the *nák > náC change is the result of a rule, currently productive in Hausa, which converts syllable final velars to C. That such a rule is productive in Hausa is seen from internal linguistic processes and from borrowings. A productive verbal derivational process reduplicates the first C_1VC_2 of a verb. If C_2 is a velar, it becomes C_1 in the reduplicated form, e.g. búgà 'beat' has the reduplicated form búbbùgà (< /búg-bùgà/), táakà 'step on' has the reduplicated form táttàakà (< /ták-tàakà/), etc. (cf. Frajzyngier 1965:32). We see the same process of *k > C in borrowings, for example líttáafìi 'book' (< *líktáafìi) borrowed from Arabic al kitābi. Yet another example of the current productivity of syllable final velar > C is in W dialects where the preposition 'from' which has the form dàgá in SH now has the form dàC (via *dàg), e.g. yáa híddà dóokìi dác cíkín dángáa 'he took the horse from within the enclosure' (see Gouffé 1968/69:9). This latter example particularly strengthens our *Cáa-kà > *Cá-k > CaC analysis since not only does it show the productivity of the rule converting syllable final velars > C, it also shows the likelihood of vowel apocopation in phonologically "weak" positions (word final, low tone, unstressed), particularly in grammatical morphemes.

Degemination

In SH, the forms náC, káC, yáC, and táC have been reduced to ná, ká, yá, and tá. That this happened is clear. What the mechanism was that brought about the change is still an open question. We could simply hypothesize that the dialect from which SH has developed never had a stage *náC, *káC, etc., i.e. there was a change directly from *nák, *kák, etc. to ná, ká, etc. While this possibility cannot be categorically ruled out, it has no obvious motivation since there are no other known cases of outright deletion of velars in similar environments. A much more plausible explanation for the SH forms is simplification of the geminate clusters at an earlier stage. We advance two possible developments. It may be that the Cá part of the Relative Perfective forms was interpreted as the pronoun so that the major constituent boundary separating C_1 and C_2 of the geminate was shifted to the left of C_1. Since Hausa does not allow initial consonant clusters of any sort, the Geminate would have automatically simplified to a single C. For example, táz-záunàa (< táC záunàa) would have been reinterpreted as tá-zzáunàa, which would have been automatically reduced to tá-záunàa 'she sat'.

Alternatively [preferred by PN], one could simply delete rather than displace the boundary between the pronominal form and the verb and treat the whole complex as a single word. Then the loss of –C would be handled by a sound change in SH which reduced all geminates to single consonants in specified phonological and/or grammatical environments,[1] e.g.

(35)   *táC-záunàa   >   *tázzáunàa   >   tázáunàa   'she sat'

Under this analysis, the interpretation of the Cá component as the PVP would be a result of, not a cause of, the reduction of the geminate into a single consonant.

---

[1] In modern Hausa, geminates are uncommon in lexical items, being (almost) entirely limited to loanwords. They occur quite commonly, on the other hand, in stems expanded by a variety of morphological processes.

Regardless of the correctness or incorrectness of any of the above hypotheses about the development of SH Relative Perfective ná, ká, tá, we wish to emphasize that these short Cá pronouns cannot be hypothesized as historically deriving directly from the short preverbal set found in other aspects. We therefore cannot agree with the suggestion of Gouffé (1966:163) that the Cá forms and the Cúkà forms of the SH Relative Perfective ". . . corresponde à une ancienne répartition des formes en fonction d'emplois syntaxiquement différents." Nor do we agree with Jungraithmayr (1968/69) who relates these Cá Relative Perfective forms to the "Grundaspekt" of other languages. The latter are historically related to the Hausa paradigm in (12). The SH Relative Perfective of Cá forms are derived by regular developments from the paradigm in (33).

Analogical Loss of n

Where W dialects have múnkà, kúnkà, súnkà, (kínkà), SH has mú-kà, kú-kà, sú-kà, kí-kà. Since the SH forms retain the unreduced kà just as do the W forms, we know that SH still used the CVN pronouns with the Relative Perfective marker at the time Vowel Apocope took place. How do we then account for the subsequent loss of the n? We described above (section 4.1) how the "free" pronouns of the form *Caa and *CVn had become specialized as markers of the Perfective aspect. With this specialization of the plural *CVn pronouns, their appearance before the overt aspect marker -kà became anomalous. Thus *mún-kà gave way to mú-kà by analogy with the standard pattern of the other aspects where overt aspect markers were found, e.g. mú-nàa, mú-kèe, mú-kàn, etc. In other words, the n as such was not actually lost in any phonological sense. Rather the pronouns with syllable final -n were replaced by members of a different pronoun set entirely. If the change of CáC to Cá (e.g. táC > tá) described above had already taken place, then the existence in the paradigm of high tone, short vowel pronouns would have provided further analogical pressure leading to the change of mún, etc. to mú, etc.

We can now summarize the developments of the Relative Perfective from early Hausa to present-day SH and W.

(36)

		Apocope	Gemination	Degemination	Analogical Loss of n	Modern Forms
SH	{ *táa-kà, etc.	tá-k	tá-C	tá		tá
	*sún-kà, etc.				sú-kà	sú-kà
W	{ *táa-kà, etc.	tá-k	tá-C			tá-C
	*sún-kà, etc.					sún-kà

In addition to the major changes described above, there have also been a couple of minor analogical changes limited to W dialects:

Analogical Replacement of kínkà by kíC:

On the basis of the SH form kí-kà and the 2f Perfective pronoun kín, one would expect the 2f Relative Perfective form in W to be kín-kà. Instead one normally finds kíC. Here we simply have a case of analogic leveling due to the fact that all the other singular pronouns are of the form CV́C (the final C being a geminate) while the plural pronouns are all of the CV́nkà. The alteration of the 2f pronoun on the model of the other singular pronouns takes place in W dialects in the neutral Perfective as well, kyáa being substituted for kín, on the model of káa 'you (m)' vs. kún 'you (pl)'. In both of these cases the usually more conservative W dialect is innovative while SH retains the reflex of the older form in kíkà.

Optional Replacement of yáC by shínkà

In Dogondoutchi, a subdialect of W, both 2f forms described in the previous paragraph (kíC and kínkà) coexist. The retention of the kínkà form completely lost elsewhere in W has been accompanied by the creation of a 3m form shínkà in competition with the normal form yáC. This form results from the replacement of ya by shi, the normal 3m PVP used in W Hausa in aspects other than the Perfective (including Negative and Relative Perfective), plus the addition of the ending -nkà by analogy with the 2f form kínkà.[1] The basis of this analogy is phonological, a contrast being drawn between pronouns with /a/ which add a geminate -C in the Relative Perfective, e.g. káC, and those with a high vowel which end in -nkà, e.g. kínkà, súnkà. Particularly interesting with regard to this innovative form is the implicit analysis of CV̌nkà forms as being made up of a CV pronoun + nkà whereas the historically accurate break is between the CV̌n pronoun and kà.

7. THE CONTINUOUS AND POTENTIAL

The Continuous aspect (also referred to as the "continuative," the "progressive," and the "inaccompli") and the Potential (or Second Future) make use of the following paradigms:

(37)		Continuous SH/W	NEG Continuous SH	W
	1	'ń-nàa/'í-nàa	báa-nàa	báa-ní
	2m	ká-nàa	" -kàa	" -ká
	2f	kí-nàa	" -kʸàa	" -kí
	3m	(yá-)nàa/(shí-)nàa	" -yàa	" -shí
	3f	(tá-)nàa	" -tàa	" -tá
	1pl	mú-nàa	" -mʷàa	" -mú
	2pl	kú-nàa	" -kʷàa	" -kú
	3pl	(sú-)nàa	" -sʷàa	" -sú
	4pl	'á-nàa	" -'àa	" -'á

(38)		Potential SH/W	Alternative in W[2]	NEG Potential
	1	náà	nîì	bà-náà . . . bá
	2m	káà	=	bà-káà . . . bá
	2f	kʸáà	kîì	etc.
	3m	yáà	shîì	
	3f	táà	=	
	1pl	mʷáà	múù	
	2pl	kʷáà	kúù	
	3pl	sʷáà	súù	
	4pl	'áà	=	

---

[1] The existence of a Perfective form shin is reported for the Sokoto dialect in a work dating from the beginning of this century (Reinisch 1909:224n).

[2] In much of the northern area, from Maradi to Zinder, the following forms are found in the

No aspect of Hausa has been the subject of as much discussion as the Continuous. Recent years have seen the publication of papers by Kraft (1964), Gregersen (1967), and Gouffé (1966/67, 1967/68) specifically devoted to this topic. The major concerns of these discussions have been the nature of the marker nàa, the obligatory use of verbal noun forms, and the question of the relation between the affirmative and negative constructions. Rather than become directly embroiled in these debates, we will proceed with a straightforward historical exposition of the Continuous. Once we have examined the modern situation from a historical point of view, the anomalies that have troubled Hausa scholars about the Continuous should begin to fall into place. We include the Continuous and Potential aspects in the same section since we believe that those two aspects can be traced back to a single Proto-Hausa source.

7.1 THE PROTO-HAUSA IMPERFECTIVE ASPECT

Before presenting the form of the Continuous in Proto-Hausa we should make two general remarks. The first is that the aspect which we are calling the "Continuous" was probably a general Imperfective in Proto-Hausa including both Continuous and Future meanings. This is a widespread phenomenon in Chadic being found, for example, in Ngizim and even in a language as close to Hausa as Gwandara.

(39)   Ngizim: nàa ráwà   'I am running' or 'I will run'

        Gwandara: mà kóm   'we are returning' or 'we will return'

If necessary, unambiguous specification of action actually in process as opposed to action in the future would have been indicated in Proto-Hausa with a quasi-aspect marker derived from a body part term used along with the Imperfective (see section 2.2 above).

Secondly, the rule requiring that at least some verbs in the Continuous be nominalized and/or replaced by a Habituative stem was undoubtedly present not only in Proto-Hausa, but must be traced back to Proto-Chadic, e.g.

(40)   Hausa: yáa kóomàa   'he returned'

                    yá-nàa kóomàa-wáa   'he is returning'

        Bolanci: ká básáa kúltí   'you shot a hare'

                    ká-n bèsè kúltí   'you are shooting a hare'

        Kanakuru: wù tìlé   'they burned it'

                    wùn tíl-mái   'they are burning it'

        Tera: tém-wà gaɓi   'we returned'

                    tém-áa gaɓtí   'we are returning'

Potential: kíǹ, múǹ, kúǹ, súǹ, 'áǹ (the remainder are the same as indicated for SH/W in 38). This information shows that the common analysis of -n as a Perfective marker (see discussion, sec. 4) cannot be sustained even in a purely synchronic description of Hausa, at least in these dialects.

7.2 RECONSTRUCTION OF THE PROTO-HAUSA IMPERFECTIVE FORMS

For Proto-Hausa, we reconstruct the Imperfective aspect paradigms in (41). Recall that the semantic range of these forms included both Continuous and Future meaning. It is from such forms that we believe both the Hausa Continuous and Potential aspects have developed.

(41)

	Affirmative	Negative
1	*náa (tone?)	*baa náa . . . bá[1]
2m	*kàa	*. . .kàa . . .
2f	*kʸàa	*. . .kʸàa . . .
3m }	∅ + *nàa	*. . .yàa (< *sàa) . . .
3f }		*. . .tàa . . .
1pl	*mʷàa	*. . .mʷàa . . .
2pl	*kʷàa	*. . .kʷàa . . .
3pl	*sʷàa (? or ∅ + *nàa)	*. . .sʷàa . . .

For most persons, the forms in these paradigms can be transparently analyzed into PVP + *àa. The high tone on first person singular is speculative. Such a tonal discrepancy in this person is found elsewhere in Chadic, e.g. in Karekare. A difference in tone between first person *náa and the *nàa seen in third person would be helpful in explaining certain developments, but is by no means crucial. The third person affirmative forms will be dealt with below.

As in the case of the Perfective, it is the present-day Negative Continuous paradigm which remains closest to the older form and the affirmative construction which has been most innovative (compare (37) with (41)). An excellent model for the reconstructed system in a present-day Chadic language is provided by Ngizim, where we find both pronouns of the Càa as well as the aspect marker àa used by itself, e.g.

(42) nàa kíɗá-k tlùwái   'I will eat (am eating) meat'

      jàa ráwà   'we will run'

      àa ráwà   'he/she/they will run'

      Dèmzà àa láuná-w   'Dəmza will see (it)'

In some respects even more significant (since we ourselves did not expect to find such striking confirmation of our reconstruction in a language so closely related to Hausa) are the following examples from Gwandara:

---

[1] We are not concerned here about the original tone of the first *baa, nor about the reason for its having a long vowel. That the Negative Imperfective had a final bá is argued in Newman (1971a) and is supported by data from Gwandara.

(43)   nà tsa kasuwa[1]   'I'm going to market'

          cf. ni kom kukundzum   'I just returned'

          ba mà yanko ba   'we are not working'

          cf. ba mu yi yanko ba   'we did not work'

          Adamu yà gba duwa   'Adamu will shoot an elephant'

          cf. Adamu ɸ ka ku   'Adamu caught a rat'

We can thus assume that Continuous sentences in Proto-Hausa (in the 1st and 2nd persons at least) would have looked something like the following:[2]

(44)   *kàa koomaawaa   'you are/will be returning'

          *baa kàa koomaawaa ba   'you are not/will not be returning'

It is the form *nàa, reconstructed for both third person masculine and femine singular and perhaps third person plural,[3] which requires some discussion and justification. Before turning to this topic, however, we wish to comment on the syntactic functions of the paradigms in (41).

There are six relevant syntactic environments. These are given in (45).

(45)	Predicate types	Constructions used with these predicates	
		Proto-Hausa Imperfective (41)	Modern Hausa Continuous (37)
	Verbal	yes	yes
	Locative	yes	yes
	'have'	no	yes
	Stative	no	yes
	Noun Phrase	no	no
	Adjective	no	no

We hypothesize that in Proto-Hausa the pronouns in question were used only with verbal or locative predicates, while in modern SH, their use has been extended to 'have' predicates (yá-nàa dà doókìi 'he has a horse') and Stative predicates (yá-nàa zàmné 'he is seated'). In Proto-Hausa, some other construction was used with 'have', Stative, Nominal and Adjectival predicates. While we cannot at present reconstruct the exact form of sentences of these types, their reflex may possibly be seen in the W morpheme 'áC, e.g. shíi 'áz zàmné 'he is seated' (Gouffé 1964:49-52). The difference in distributions of predicate types between Proto-Hausa and modern Hausa can be deduced on internal grounds from the use of two different

---

[1] [PN] Because of the field circumstances under which the Gwandara data were collected, I have little confidence in my transcription of tone except for the Imperfective pronouns which were unmistakably low. Phonemic vowel length in Gwandara seems to have been lost.

[2] In hypothetical sentences, tones are marked only for pronouns and aspect markers.

[3] To simplify the exposition we will assume that Proto-Hausa allowed either *sʷàa or ɸ + *nàa as options in the affirmative. The crux of our argument is in no way dependent on this assumption.

negative forms but only one affirmative in SH (see section 7.2.3). Stronger evidence comes from comparison with other languages. For example, the distribution cited in (45) for Proto-Hausa is found in Ngizim and Karekare.[1]

7.2.1 The Origin of Third Person nàa

The reconstruction of an Imperfective *aa is based on widespread comparative evidence. Our reconstruction of a special third person *naa is based on evidence from the Bole group of languages, which is the Chadic subgroup most closely related to Hausa. Karekare furnishes a situation very much like that reconstructed for the Proto-Hausa affirmative in (41). In Karekare there is a marker náa, used only in locative and Imperfective verbal constructions, for all third persons. This marker is possible when there is a noun subject or where no overt subject is expressed. Since no distinction is made for gender and number, a sentence such as (46) is three ways ambiguous out of context:

(46)   náa ɗə́bátúu tò   'he/she/they are selling it'

Náa cannot be used together with a pronoun subject nor can it be used in first or second person. If it is felt necessary to overtly express gender or number in third person, the pronominal elements sàa (3 sg.m.), tàa (3 sg.f.), sáa (pl) can substitute for the náa. Thus, the following sentences are found in Lukas (1966:180–181). Both can be seen to have plural subjects from context, but in (b) the phrase bòo wáɗí "together" (lit: 'one mouth') would make the plural pronoun, sáa, redundant.[2]

(47)   (a) sáa zù màrkó   'they were traveling'

          (b) náa zù màrkó bòo wáɗí   'they were traveling together'

Proto-Hausa may likewise have had the option of substituting *yàa ~ *sàa, *tàa, or *sᵂàa for ø + *nàa as a means of disambiguating gender and number. There is no internal evidence in Hausa to shed light on this question.

Kanakuru also has an Imperfective morpheme nàa. Probably as a result of independent Kanakuru developments, the distribution of this morpheme is somewhat different from that of Karekare or Proto-Hausa. In Kanakuru, nàa is used in the Imperfective if the subject of the sentence has been moved from preverbal position. Typically, this will be the case when a subject has been moved to post-verbal position for emphasis. Unlike Karekare and Proto-Hausa, Kanakuru nàa is used in all persons.

(48)   ø nàa wúpé lándài shíjí   'you (f) are selling/will sell the gown'

          cf. shìjì wúpé lándài   'you (f) are selling the gown'

          cf. ø wùpè̀ lándài shíjí   'you (f) sold the gown'

          (no nàa since aspect is not Imperfective)

---

[1] It is interesting to note that in Kanakuru, the construction corresponding to Hausa Continuous has been extended to all the predicate types in (45) (see Newman 1973). We can recognize this as an independent Kanakuru development, however, since among the languages cited in this connection—Hausa, Ngizim, Karekare, Kanakuru—Kanakuru is most closely related to Karekare, a language having a distribution like that given for Proto-Hausa.

[2] In (47) (a) and (b), the word zù 'body' is used as a quasi-Continuous aspect marker. As in many other Chadic languages, the bare Imperfective in Karekare covers the whole range of progressive and future meaning.

Note that the use of nàa in Kanakuru in all persons is a natural extension of its use elsewhere if our analysis of *nàa for Proto-Hausa (and probably for Proto-Bole-Hausa) is correct, viz. *nàa is actually a marker used in the absence of a special preverbal pronominal form. (Recall that typically, Chadic languages have no special preverbal pronoun in third person.) Presumably in synchronic grammars of Proto-Hausa and Karekare, the rule inserting naa would be an early transformation and would be blocked in first and second person where pronominal subjects would be present. In a synchronic Kanakuru grammar, nàa insertion can be interpreted as a late rule, ordered after rules which remove subjects from preverbal position. The rule inserting nàa will thus be pretty much the same in Kanakuru as in Proto-Hausa or Karekare. Its function is simply extended as a result of its relatively late application.

It seems evident that the third person naa which we have been discussing is analyzable at some synchronic or diachronic level into n- + -aa. As mentioned in section 2.1, ni is a very common third person masculine singular pronoun form in Chadic.[1] However, we must consider the *nàa reconstructed for Proto-Hausa to be an unanalyzable unit. In the Bole Cluster languages cited, naa certainly functions in this unitary fashion, as does the nàa Continuous marker of modern Hausa. If we reconstructed Proto-Hausa as having *nàa analyzable into *n- + *-aa, we would have to claim that Karekare, Kanakuru, and Hausa all independently innovated by creating unit "naa's" from n- + -aa.

7.2.2 The Adoption and Spread of nàa in Hausa

Returning now to our reconstructed paradigms in (41), we can distinguish, in effect, two Imperfective markers in complementary distribution: *nàa in third person and *àa elsewhere. Our contention is that *nàa, restricted to third person in Proto-Hausa, was reinterpreted as being a general marker of Imperfective aspect and was consequently extended to all persons. This took place only in the affirmative since in Proto-Hausa, third person *nàa was not used in the negative.

There are several possible mechanisms by which this extension of the use of *nàa could have taken place:

One possibility is that the third person PVP's were, at some stage, optionally prefixed to *nàa for disambiguation of number and gender. The result would have been interpretable as a construction of the form PVP + aspect marker. As speakers lost sight of the fact that *nàa itself incorporated the third person feature as well as the aspect feature, it was reinterpreted as being simply the aspect marker and extended to use with the PVP's of first and second person. However, this hypothesis raises the question of why gender or number would have been disambiguated by PVP's rather than, say, substituting for *nàa the unitary forms *yàa, *tàa, and *sʷàa already available (cf. the Karekare data above).

A second possibility is a push-chain effect cause by the anomalous tone of the first person singular. If indeed this person had a tone different from all other persons, there would have been analogical pressure to bring it into line with the other persons. However, a change of tone in first person *náa would make it homophonous with third person *nàa. To avoid ambiguity, the PVP's would have been added before third person *nàa. Use of PVP + *nàa would have then spread to other persons as suggested above. The weakness of this hypothesis is in the admittedly speculative claim that first person singular had an anomalous tone. (However, as we mentioned above, there is some comparative support for this.) There is also the problem already noted, viz. why would PVP's have been used rather than the forms *yàa, *tàa, and *sʷàa.

---

[1] Gouffé (1970/71) has also documented the existence in West Africa outside of Chadic of a marker *N- with apparently similar functions to *n- found in Chadic Imperfective formations. What significance this has (if any) with regard to the origin and development of Hausa nàa remains to be established.

A third possibility is that the contemporary structure of PVP + nàa did not result from extension of the use of PVP's from third person to other persons at all. As we have argued, presence of *nàa in Proto-Hausa would have been triggered by the absence of an overt pronominal subject, i.e. it was restricted to use after non-pronominal NP or ϕ. If this restriction were simply removed, then the automatic consequence would have been the introduction of *nàa as the AUX in all persons. While this solution avoids the problems with the two preceding suggestions, it begs the question of what the actual mechanism might have been for removal of the restriction on the environments where *nàa could appear.

We cannot now say with confidence which, if any, of the above hypotheses on the spread of *nàa is correct. We are, however, confident of the correctness of our reconstruction of the Hausa Continuous markers. That is, Proto-Hausa had a marker *àa used in all but third person and a marker *nàa used only in third person (and probably only in the affirmative). It is this special third person *nàa which appears today in all persons as a Continuous aspect marker. We might also note that sentences like màcè nàa fìtáa 'the woman is going out', where optionally nàa is used after a non-pronominal NP without a PVP, is a reflex of the Proto-Hausa situation. The usual descriptions of such sentences imply that the pronoun is optionally dropped, e.g. Maxwell and Forshey (n.d.:66) say, "The continuous forms yana, tana, and suna are often contracted to na simply." This may be the best way to describe the construction synchronically, but from a diachronic point of view, such constructions represent non-insertion of a PVP.

7.2.3 Contemporary Forms of the Negative Continuous

The affirmative Continuous has seen extension of more restricted constructions to more general use in two ways: first, a formative *nàa, originally restricted to use in third person, has been extended to become the continuous marker in all persons; second, the entire affirmative Continuous paradigm, originally restricted to use with verbal and locative predicates, has been extended to use with 'have' and stative predicates.

In both these senses, the Negative Continuous has been more conservative. In SH, the Negative Continuous báa-tàa forms have continued virtually unchanged in form from the Proto-Hausa reconstructions in (41). Moreover the Negative Continuous has retained a syntactic distribution closer to that reconstructed for Proto-Hausa than has affirmative Continuous. In SH 'have' sentences use negative constructions of the form báa-tá rather than the Negative Continuous báa-tàa.[1] We suggested above that the Proto-Hausa 'have' and stative constructions find a modern affirmative reflex in the W 'áC forms. The negative counterpart of the 'áC affirmative is the Falling-Hi báa-tá forms. Thus, in one dialect area at least (SH), the older syntactic distribution is more closely maintained in the negative than it is in the affirmative.

Even without dialectal and cross-language evidence, we can infer on universal typological grounds that the modern SH Continuous must have formerly been expressed by two separate affirmative construction types. The universal rule is that there are always fewer formal distinctions in the negative than in the affirmative (or else an equal number). The diachronic implication of this is that a negative *báa-tàa could not split into syntactically distinct negatives báa-tàa and báa-tá while the affirmative utilized only one form. The explanation must therefore be that two separate affirmative constructions have merged, leaving distinct the negatives with which they were paired.

---

[1] Contrary to what our hypothesis predicts, the báa-yàa forms rather than the báa-shí forms are used with stative predicates. This could result through spread from verbal predicates because of the verb-like nature of statives. Whatever the explanation, realignments are to be expected because of the instability inherent in a situation where affirmative forms are paired with dissimilar negatives.

Another implication of this fact of universal typology is that a situation with one affirmative paired with two negatives is unstable. This instability is clearly seen in modern Hausa. In W, the old báa-tàa forms have now been completely replaced in all constructions by the báà-tá forms. In SH there is a definite tendency among some speakers to replace the báà-tá forms in 'have' constructions by báa-tàa. The result in both W and SH is a return to the stable situation of one negative paired with one affirmative.

Gouffé (1967/68: 48-50) has suggested that SH has innovated by replacing the short, high-tone pronouns in báà-tá by the long, low-tone pronouns in báa-tàa by phonological analogy with the long, low-tone nàa of the affirmative (perhaps through confusion of this nàa with the first person singular pronoun). Above, we have given our reasons for believing that the SH báa-tàa forms represent the older state. From our position, it follows that W has innovated by a syntactic replacement of the báa-tàa forms by báà-tá.[1] By contrast, negatives such as báa-tà, given for DD by Zima (1967), can be said to be phonologically derived from báà-tá by a minor change whereby the uncommon Falling-Hi sequence is replaced by the more common Hi-Lo pattern.

7.2.4 The Potential and Negative Potential

We can assume that even after third person *nàa had begun to be extended to use with other persons, the older, unitary forms *kàa, *tàa, etc. remained in use as well. When two forms — in this case *tá-nàa and *tàa — occupy the same semantic ground, one of two developments is certain: one of the forms will be lost entirely, or the semantic space will be divided with each form taking on a more restricted meaning. Recall that the Proto-Hausa Imperfective has been reconstructed as covering the entire semantic area of progressive and future action. There was plenty of semantic space to accomodate a split in function, and in time, the *tàa forms came to denote futurity, the *tá-nàa forms progressive action.

Once the former Continuous, now Potential, paradigm *kàa, *kʸàa, *tàa, etc. was re-interpreted as a distinct aspect in its own right, it was moulded phonologically and syntactically to fit into the general pattern of the Hausa aspect system. Phonologically, the anomalous low tone on the long vowel was replaced by a falling tone in line with the preferred high-low pattern for sequences of short vowel PVP + aspect marker (cf. the present form of the Potential tá-à with the Continuous tá-nàa).

In line with its semantic shift and its separation from the Continuous, the Potential dropped the use of the Negative Continuous set (báa-kàa, etc.) which it had shared with the nàa Continuous and formed a new negative using the productive bà. . .bá construction, e.g. bà táà 'íyàa bá 'she probably will not be able'. With this new negative construction for the Potential, the old Negative Imperfective (báa-tàa, etc.) was left to be paired exclusively with the new nàa affirmative Continuous.

Finally, the Potential completed its development as a separate aspect belonging to the general aspect system by discarding the Continuous rule which requires that finite verbs be altered into verbal noun forms, e.g.

(49)	Potential	yáà zóo	'he will probably come'
	NEG Continuous	báa yàa zúwàa	'he is not coming'

---

[1] Gouffé, in personal communication to PN, gives the parallelism between W Continuous and W Future as one reason for believing that the W báà tá forms represent the more conservative state. In W both these constructions have the form Cáà-CV́ + verbal noun. However, parallelism really says nothing about conservatism, and in fact, one might suggest that W replaced báa tàa by báà tá in order to make the Continuous parallel with the Future. We give a straightforward explanation of the modern Hausa Future in section 9.

While the historical analysis of the Negative Continuous and Potential pronouns of the form C a a is transparently PVP + à a, the functional value of this analysis must have been discarded by Hausa speakers fairly early. Vowel length and tone have now largely taken over the function(s) of the older bi-morphemic analysis. This is clearly evidenced by the replacement in much of the Hausa-speaking area of the C a a forms by forms having the vowel qualities of the Independent Pronouns or even replacement of the Potential C á à forms by pronouns formally identical to the Perfective pronouns but with falling tone (see p. 23, (37) and fn. 2).

See Table 1 for a summary of the development of the Continuous and Potential aspects.

8.   THE RELATIVE CONTINUOUS

The Relative Continuous substitutes for the Continuous in exactly the same syntactic environments in which the Relative Perfective replaces the Perfective.[1] The two Continuous forms are semantically equivalent and in syntactically determined complementary distribution. The Relative Continuous paradigms in modern Hausa are as follows:

(50)   SH   W

1	ná-kèe	ní-kà
2m	ká-kèe	ká-kà
2f	kî-kèe	kí-kà
3m	(yá-)kèe	(shí-)kà
3f	(tá-)kèe	(tá-)kà
1pl	mú-kèe	mú-kà
2pl	kú-kèe	kú-kà
3pl	(sú-)kèe	(sú-)kà
4pl	'á-kèe	'á-kà

8.1 THE ORIGIN OF THE RELATIVE CONTINUOUS

The syntactic alternation between a Relative Perfective and a regular Perfective is widespread in Chadic and is probably reconstructable for Proto-Chadic. Hausa is unique in Chadic — as far as we are aware — in also having a relative construction corresponding to a neutral construction in the Continuous. In trying to historically explain the existence of the Relative Continuous in Hausa, therefore, we must assume that it arose within Hausa itself. Our hypothesis is that the complementarity of the two Continuous aspects was created by syntactic analogy with the Perfective/Relative Perfective alternation. We believe, moreover, following Gouffé (1966/67: 59) that the kèe/kà Relative Continuous markers are actually derived from the same *kà morpheme that we reconstructed as the Relative Perfective marker in Proto-Hausa and which is still partially retained in that function in contemporary Hausa.

As we described earlier, the Proto-Plateau-Sahel Perfective marker *kà had already come to

---

[1]"Il suffira alors de dire que l'Accompli II et l'Inaccompli II sont formes par lesquelles s'expriment normalement (du moins en haoussa 'standard') les aspects accompli et inaccompli lorsqu'ils doivent apparaître dans une portion d'énoncé de type 'subordonné' " (Gouffé 1966: 159).

Table 1 - Summary of the Development of Hausa Continuous and Potential

Proto-Hausa	Extension of *nàa	Split of Imperfective Functions	Phon. Change	Split of Negative	Negative Neutralization	Modern Hausa
Imperfective Affirmative						
*Càa [1]	*Càa	Poten.: *Càa ⟶ Cáà			⟶ táà
∅ + *nàa	PVP + *nàa ⟶ Cont.: PVP + nàa				⟶ tá-nàa
Imperfective Negative						
		bà Cáà...bá		bà táà...bá	
*baa Càa...ba		bâa Càa³ ⟶ bâa Càa; báà-C✓		(SH) báa tàa / (W) báá tá
Non-Verbal[2] Negative						
? *báà C✓		⟶ báà C✓, báa Càa			(SH) báá tà / báà tàa / báà tá (W) báá tà / báà tá

some SH

W

Only the major developments are summarized here. Minor phonological realignments such as DD báa-tà < bâa-tà or W Potential múu < mwâa, etc. are omitted. We also have omitted the extension of the -nàa Continuous from its original restriction to use with verbal and locative sentences to use with 'have' and stative predicates.

---

[1] The ∅ + *nàa forms were used only in third person, the *Càa forms elsewhere.

[2] It is not certain what the exact form was. We have hypothesized that the affirmative counterpart has a reflex in W ʼáC. We are able to say nothing about the history of this affirmative form other than that it was replaced at some point in SH by the nàa Continuous in some functions.

[3] At some point, the Proto-Hausa *baa...ba was replaced by báa. It is not possible to determine where this took place relative to the other changes.

be a Relative Perfective marker in Proto-Hausa. It is not difficult to imagine, then, how this marker could be further reinterpreted as simply a "relative morpheme" ("un morphème de subordination"), i.e. as a marker of relative/subordinate environments without specific limitation as to aspect. For example, after the free pronouns were established as the Perfective set (see section 4.1 above), the Relative Perfective form *mún-kà would naturally have been analyzed as *mún '1pl Perfective' + *kà 'relative marker'. The extension of this relative marker into the Continuous as a replacement for nàa would have given *mú-kà '1pl Relative Continuous' — exactly what we find in W Hausa today. The surface difference in SH between the two relative forms, kà (Perfective) and kèe (Continuous) would then be due to a minor vowel shift affecting only the latter — for which we have no satisfactory explanation — paralleled elsewhere in SH by the change in the stabilizers naa and taa to nee and cee. (The long vowel of SH kèe as opposed to the short vowel of W kà follows from the fact that e in Hausa is normally long. Short e does occur but only as a result of specific phonological or morphological conditioning.) Note that as a result of the split of *kà into kà and kèe, the marker kà in SH can no longer be considered as an aspectually neutral relative morpheme. In other words, unless our analysis itself is wrong, we find the interesting situation in SH of contemporary kà having recovered its original connection with the Perfective which was supposed to have been lost at some intermediate stage.

Without getting involved in a discussion of non-verbal sentences we would like to comment briefly on the morpheme kè used in the Tibiri, Dogondoutchi, and other subdialects of W in locative and 'have' sentences (see Gouffé 1966/67:58ff.). While it would be tempting to derive this form from the relative marker *kà and thus connect it with the kà/kèe Relative Continuous markers, we feel that this analysis is wrong. Rather, we agree with Gouffé (1966/67:60-63), who identifies W kè as a syntactic alternate of 'áC (kè and 'áC are partly in complementary distribution, partly in free (?) variation). The resemblance of the relative markers kà/kèe to the kè which pairs with 'áC is fortuitous, the latter probably being cognate with the Gwandara equational marker ko. Note that the syntactic distinction between W kè/'áC and W Relative Continuous kà further supports our contention that early Hausa distinguished a Continuous aspect (*Càa) and a non-verbal construction type (now 'áC).[1]

---

[1] Syntactic complementary distribution according to predicate types is not the only feature distinguishing W kè and W Relative Continuous kà. Gouffé reports (1966/67:61) that the Relative Continuous kà may be used in the third person without a PVP, e.g. shíi nàa (shí) kà cín náamàa 'it is he who is eating meat', whereas the marker kè requires a pronominal prefix in all environments, e.g. shíi nàa shí-kè gàríi 'it is he who is in town', but not *shíi nàa kè gàríi. (The nàa in these examples is the W form of the stabilizer, not the Continuous morpheme.) Probably more significant is an observation made by Gouffé (to PN in personal communication) that SH also recognizes a morpheme kè, found in exactly the same environments as W kè! We eagerly await further information on this heretofore unobserved fact.

9. THE FUTURE

The paradigms used in the Future are as follows:

(51) (a)   SH   (b)   W

1	zá-ǹ (< záa-nì)	záà-ní
2m	záa-kà	záà-ká
2f	záa-kì	záà-kí
3m	zá-ỳ (< záa-yà)	záà-shí
3f	záa-tà	záà-tá
1pl	záa-mù	záà-mú
2pl	záa-kù	záà-kú
3pl	záa-sù	záà-sú
4pl	záa-'à	záà-'á

In the negative, SH uses bà...bá with the forms in (a). W uses the Negative Continuous.

In verbal sentences SH uses paradigm (51a) followed by finite verbs, W uses paradigm (51b) followed by verbal noun forms or, less often, by finite verbs. Both dialects use paradigm (51b) when immediately followed by a locative goal, e.g.

(52)   SH: záa-mù cí náamàa   ⎫
                                              ⎬ 'we will eat meat'
         W: záà-mú cíǹ náamàa   ⎭

         SH and W: záà-mú kàasúwáa   'we're going to market'

9.1 ANALYSIS OF THE W PARADIGM

Hausa scholars have long recognized that the Future is a paraphrastic construction using the verbal form záà/záa meaning 'to go' rather than a simple aspect formed with a regular aspect marker. The position and form of the pronouns, however, have presented more of a problem in analysis. Parsons (1960/61) considers the pronouns in paradigm (51b) as obligatorily postposed subject pronouns. Gouffé (1967/68) correctly rejects Parsons' analysis of these pronouns as subjects but then is misled by their phonological shape into labeling them as direct objects. The proper analysis of these pronouns suggests itself when verbal systems of related languages are considered. In a number of Chadic languages one finds the use of a pronominal suffix on verbs which Newman (1971b, 1973) has called the ICP ('Intransitive Copy Pronoun'). This ICP which agrees in person, number, and gender with the subject, is suffixed to intransitive (and only intransitive) verbs. Consider the following paradigm from Kanakuru:

(53)   1   nà tà-nó   'I went'   cf. nà túi   'I ate'
         2m   kà tà-kó   'you (m) . . .'   à nái   'he/she drank'
         2f   shì tà-shí   'you (f) . . .'
         3m   à tà-ní   'he . . .'
         3f   à tà-tó   'she . . .'

1pl	mè tà-mú	'we . . .'
2pl	kè tà-kú	'you (pl) . . .'
3pl	wù tà-wú	'they . . .'

In Kanakuru the ICP is used with all intransitive verbs whether functioning as main verbs or as auxiliaries, e. g.

(54)   à ɗùwò-tó   'she remained/she sat'

cf. (à) ɗùwò-tó shír-mái   'she habitually steals'

An even more striking example of ICP usage with an intransitive verb in an auxiliary capacity is the Future construction in Ngamo (examples from Jungraithmayr 1970b):

(55)   nè gónnó tìishê   'I will eat'   'cf. nè tù-kô   'I ate'

kò gótkó . . .   'you (m) . . .'   (kô is a Perfective marker,
                                              not an ICP)
shì gɓooshí . . .   'you (f) . . .'

'à gónní . . .   'he . . .'

'à góotó . . .   'she . . .'

We conclude, therefore, that the pronouns suffixed to záà in the Hausa future are ICP's which have been retained in spite of the loss of ICP attachment as a productive process in Hausa.[1] A major Hausa innovation as compared with the Ngamo paradigm (55) has been the obligatory deletion of the subject pronouns in the environment of záà + ICP. In Kanakuru, deletion of the subject pronoun is also required (or nearly so) with the verbally derived auxiliary ɗuwo plus ICP, e.g.

(56)   *nà ɗùwò-nó nái méèn   →   ɗùwò-nó nái méèn
                                        'I habitually/customarily drink beer'

à ɗùwò-tó shír-mái   →   ɗùwò-tó shír-mái
                                        'she habitually steals'

9.2 THE DEVELOPMENT OF THE SH FUTURE

We have assumed all along, as Gouffé (1967/68) has done for separate reasons, that the W Future represents the older form and that the SH construction is derived from it. This change can be explained in the following manner.

Originally a sentence such as (ni) záà-ní sàyén náamàa would have meant 'I'm going (in order) to buy meat' (more literally 'I'm going (for) buying meat') and would have had a constituent structure as represented in the following diagram:

---

[1]Vestiges of the old ICP's still remain in a few fossilized forms such as jèe-ká 'go!' and yáa-kà 'come here!'.

(57)

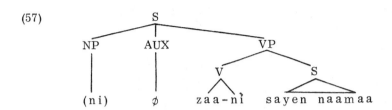

With the loss of the ICP attachment rule (which had overtly marked záà as a verb) and a gradual shift in the meaning of such constructions from 'in order to' to straight futurity, the sentence in (57) was altered into a sentence with a structure as illustrated in the following diagram:

(58)

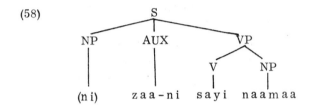

In SH, the change to the structure in (58) was accompanied by two changes, one phonological, the other syntactic, designed to create a construction compatible with the reanalysis of the záà + ICP as an AUX. One change was the adoption of the normal high-low tone pattern for the AUX, the former ICP pronouns giving way to the PVP set, e.g. záà-mú > záa-mù and záà-shí > záa-yà. The other change was the substitution of finite verbs for nominalized verbs by analogy with the other aspects (see example (52)). Note that both of these changes were paralleled by identical changes in the Potential as well.

10.   SUMMARY

We have reconstructed the formal characteristics of the verbal aspect system of Proto-Hausa, showing how our reconstructed system has evolved through a series of plausible stages into the system(s) seen in contemporary Hausa dialects. Our orientation in explaining the contemporary forms has been diachronic, but certainly there are a number of implications for a synchronic description of Hausa.

Unlike previous investigations of Hausa diachrony, which have relied exclusively on internal reconstruction, our approach has relied heavily on comparison of Hausa with closely related Chadic languages. This comparative approach has given us the advantage of viewing the internal anomalies of Hausa in a new light.

We began with a rather schematically reconstructed aspect marking system for Proto-Chadic. This consisted of a Preverbal Pronoun (PVP) plus an aspect marker plus a verb stem. The PVP was reconstructed as a short pronominal form of the shape CV which had as its only function the marking of person, number, and gender. Its tone was determined by phonological factors. Aspect itself was marked by the presence of an aspect marker (we reconstructed *kà Perfective, ∅ "Grundaspekt," *àa Imperfective) plus changes in the verb stem for some aspects, e.g. tonal shifts and/or different vocalic suffixes. While no Chadic language to our knowledge preserves this system in exactly this form, all Chadic languages to a greater or lesser extent bear witness to its prior existence. Hausa is no exception.

With this Proto-Chadic system as our basis for the reconstruction of Proto-Hausa, we have been able to advance a number of hypotheses about the evolution of Hausa. Briefly summarized, our principal hypotheses are the following:

(1) Proto-Hausa had a series of low tone, short vowel pronouns (PVP) which marked person, number, and gender of the subject, but which had no independent aspect-marking function.

(2) The modern Perfective aspect pronouns having the form Cáa or CV́n did not evolve from the Proto-Hausa PVP. Rather, they represent a paradigm of unbound pronouns which has developed an aspect marking function since the time of Proto-Hausa.

(3) The short, low tone pronominal elements in the modern Hausa Negative Perfective are reflexes of Proto-Hausa Perfective, both affirmative and negative. Both the modern Negative Perfective and the modern Subjunctive pronouns are reflexes of the bare PVP of Proto-Hausa. In Proto-Hausa Subjunctive and Perfective were distinguished by differences in final vowel and/or tone of the verb stem.

(4) A transformation substituting Relative Perfective for Perfective in certain syntactic contexts is reconstructed for Proto-Hausa. The Proto-Hausa Relative Perfective was composed of Perfective pronouns very similar to the modern Perfective series plus a marker *kà. The modern Hausa reflexes of this reconstruction are the result of natural phonological developments.

(5) The modern Continuous and Potential aspects have evolved from a single Proto-Hausa aspect, the Imperfective. As in the Perfective, the modern reflex of the Proto-Hausa construction is best preserved in the negative, seen as the long, low tone Càa (< PVP + *àa) pronouns of SH Negative Continuous. The modern -nàa Continuous marker comes from extension of the use of an invariable Imperfective marker *nàa, originally restricted to third person where no overt pronoun subject was present. Use of PVP + nàa is thus an innovation since the time of Proto-Hausa.

(6) The modern Potential is a reflex of the Proto-Hausa *Càa Imperfective constructions, which were specialized to a futurity meaning. This semantic specialization was possible because the spread of Imperfective *nàa to first and second persons yielded two co-existent possibilities for Imperfective: *Càa or PVP + *nàa.

(7) SH Negative Continuous báa-Càa is a reflex of Proto-Hausa Negative Imperfective; the modern Hausa báà-CV́ negative, now paired in some cases with affirmative Continuous, is the reflex of the negative construction used in non-verbal sentences; modern Hausa bà Cáa . . . bá Negative Potential is a new formation created to pair with the modern Potential.

(8) The modern transformation substituting Relative Continuous for Continuous in certain contexts is an innovation based on analogy with the transformation making a similar substitution in the Perfective. The original Relative Continuous marker was *kà, still seen in W. SH kèe is a later, purely phonological innovation.

(9) The záa- Future is paraphrastic in origin, coming from the verb záà- 'go'. The pronominal suffixes to this verb are a vestige of a common Chadic phenomenon whereby a pronominal copy of the subject is added to intransitive verbs.

11. REFERENCES

Abbreviations

AuÜ   Afrika und Übersee
GLECS   Comptes rendus du groupe linguistique d'études chamito-sémitiques
JAL   Journal of African Languages
SAL   Studies in African Linguistics, UCLA
ZfES   Zeitschrift für Eingeborenen-Sprachen

Abraham, R.C. 1959. The Language of the Hausa People. London: University of London
    Press.

Eulenberg, John B. 1967. The Syntax of the Hausa Subject Prefixes. Unpublished master's
    thesis, Harvard University.

Frajzyngier, Zygmunt. 1965. 'An Analysis of Intensive Forms in Hausa Verbs.' Rocznik
    Orientalistyczny 29:31-51.

Gouffé, Claude. 1964. 'A propos de la phrase relative et de la phrase nominale en berbère
    et en haoussa.' GLECS 10:35-54.

_____. 1966. 'Les problèmes de l'aspect en haoussa. I - Introduction. Le problème
    de l'Aoriste et de l'Accompli II.' GLECS 10:151-165.

_____. 1966/67. 'Les problèmes de l'aspect en haoussa. II - Le problème de
    l'Inaccompli I et II.' GLECS 11:29-67.

_____. 1967/68. 'Les problèmes de l'aspect en haoussa. III - l'Inaccompli négatif
    et l'Ingressif.' GLECS 12/13:27-51.

_____. 1968/69. 'Deux notes grammaticales sur le parler haoussa de Dogondoutchi
    (République du Niger).' AuÜ 52:1-14.

_____. 1970/71. 'Une correlation typologique dans quatre langues de l'Afrique
    occidentale: les fonctions de *N-.' AuÜ 54:286-302.

Gregersen, Edgar A. 1967. 'Some Competing Analyses in Hausa.' JAL 6:42-57.

Hoffmann, Carl. 1971. 'Provisional Check List of Chadic Languages.' Chadic Newsletter,
    Marburg.

Jungraithmayr, Herrmann. 1964/65. 'Die Sprache der Sura (Maghavul) in Nordnigerien.'
    AuÜ 47:8-89,204-220.

_____. 1966. 'Zum Bau der Aspekte im Westtschadohamitischen.'
    Z. der Deutschen Morgenländischen Gesellschaft 116:227-234.

_____. 1968/69. 'Hausa, Ron, and Angas: a comparative analysis of their
    'aspect' systems.' AuÜ 52:15-22.

_____. 1970a. Die Ron-Sprachen: Tschadohamitische Studien in Nordnigerien.
    Glückstadt: Afrikanistische Forschungen 3.

_____. 1970b. 'Types of Conjugational Forms in Chadic.' Paper presented
    at the Colloquium on Hamito-Semitic Comparative Linguistics, London, March 18-20,
    1970.

Klingenheben, August. 1927/28. 'Die Silbenauslautgesetze des Hausa.' ZfES 18:272-297.

_____. 1928/29. 'Die Tempora Westafrikas und die Semitischen Tempora.'
ZfES 19: 241-268.

Kraft, Charles. 1964. 'The Morpheme nà in Relation to a Broader Classification of Hausa
Verbals.' JAL 3:231-240.

_____. 1972. 'Reconstruction of Chadic Pronouns.' Paper presented at the Third
Annual Conference on African Linguistics, Bloomington, April 6-8, 1972.

Leben, William R. 1971. 'The Morphophonemics of Tone in Hausa.' In Chin-Wu Kim and
Herbert Stahlke (eds.), Papers in African Linguistics, pp. 201-218. Edmonton,
Alberta: Linguistic Research, Inc.

Lukas, Johannes. 1937/38. 'Der Hamitische Gehalt der Tschadohamitischen Sprachen.' ZfES
28:286-299.

_____. 1966. 'Tschadohamitische Sprachproben aus Nordnigerien (Karekare- und
Bolanci-Texte).' in J. Lukas (ed.). Neue Afrikanistische Studien, pp. 173-207.
Hamburg.

_____. 1970-72. 'Die Personalia und das primäre Verb im Bolanci (Nordnigerien).
Mit Beiträgen über das Karekare.' AuÜ 54:237-286, 55:114-139.

Maxwell, J. Lowry and Eleanor M. Forshey. n.d. Yau da Gobe. A Hausa Grammar for
Beginners. Lagos.

Newman, Paul. 1970. 'Historical Sound Laws in Hausa and in Dera (Kanakuru).' J. West
Afr. Lang. 7:39-51.

_____. 1971a. 'The Hausa Negative Markers.' SAL 2:183-195.

_____. 1971b. 'Transitive and Intransitive in Chadic Languages.' In Veronika Six,
et. al. (eds.), Afrikanische Sprachen und Kulturen - Ein Querschnitt, pp. 188-200.
Hamburg: Hamburger Beiträge Zur Afrika-Kunde 14.

_____. 1972. 'Syllable Weight as a Phonological Variable.' SAL 3:301-323.

_____. 1973. The Kanakuru Language. West African Language Monograph No. 9 (in press).

Newman, Paul and Roxana Ma. 1966. 'Comparative Chadic: Phonology and Lexicon.' JAL 5:218-251.

Parsons, F.W. 1960/61. 'The Verbal System in Hausa.' AuÜ 44:1-36.

_____. 1965. 'Towards a Transformational Grammar of Hausa.' Unpublished paper
presented at the Fifth West African Language Congress, University of Ghana,
5-10 April 1965.

Reinisch, Leo. 1909. Das Persönliche Fürwort und die Verbalflexion in den Chamito-
semitischen Sprachen. Vienna: Alfred Hölder.

Schuh, Russell G. 1971. 'Verb Forms and Verb Aspects in Ngizim.' In Paul Newman (ed.).
'Special Chadic Issue.' JAL 10:47-60.

Zima, Petr. 1969. 'A Contribution to the Analysis of Verbal Forms in a WNW Hausa Dialect.'
Archiv Orientálni, Warsaw 37:199-213.